I Love Chinese

wǒ ài huá
我 爱 华 语

WORKBOOK
练 习 册

www.BetterChinese.com

 I Love Chinese

I Love Chinese Workbook
Simplified Chinese Characters

Copyright © 2012 Better World Ltd.

All rights reserved. No part of this publication may be adapted, reproduced, stored in a retrieval system or transmitted in any form or by any means, electronic, mechanical, photocopying, recording, or otherwise without permission from the publisher.

Founder: Li-hsiang Yu 虞丽翔
Publisher: Chi-kuo Shen 沈启国
Illustrations by Better World Ltd.
Published by Better World Ltd.
1 2 3 XLA 15 14 13

P. O. Box 695
Palo Alto, CA 94302, USA

Tel: +1-650-384-0902

Email: usa@betterchinese.com

Web: www.BetterChinese.com

Use this product with our Online Learning System at www.BetterChinese.com.

ISBN-13: 978-1-60603-093-6
ISBN-10: 1-60603-093-0

第一册 Book 1	你好 Greetings	………………………………1
第二册 Book 2	这是什么形状? What Shape Is This?	………………………………5
第三册 Book 3	你想做什么? What Do You Want To Be?	………………………………9
第四册 Book 4	你去哪里? Where Are You Going?	………………………………13
第五册 Book 5	一年四季 Four Seasons	………………………………17
第六册 Book 6	真好吃 It's So Delicious!	………………………………21

目录 / Contents

第七册 Book 7	动物 Animals	26
第八册 Book 8	虫虫飞 The Insect Flew Away	30
第九册 Book 9	大海里有什么？ What's In The Ocean?	34
第十册 Book 10	我们一起打球 Let's Play Ball Together	39
第十一册 Book 11	我喜欢交朋友 I Like Making Friends	43
第十二册 Book 12	我好棒 I Am Great!	47
剪贴页 Cut and Paste		51

 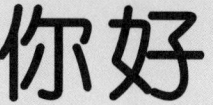

1

Exercise 1: Matchmaker

Link the pictures with the correct phrases.

   •   • bú kè qi
　　　　　　　　　　不客气

   •   • méi guān xi
　　　　　　　　　　没关系

   •   • yí huìr jiàn
　　　　　　　　　　一会儿见

 •   • nǐ hǎo
　　　　　　　　　　你好

1

 你好

Exercise 2: Fun With Stroke Orders

Color the strokes in the order they are numbered. Then use the characters in the sentence below.

____好！ 跟____来。

 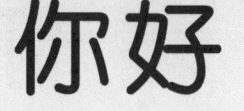

1

Exercise 3: Word Puzzle
Circle the following words in the puzzle.

你好
谢谢你
不客气
再见
加油
没关系
对不起

加	你	谢	谢	你
没	油	对	我	好
关	有	不	客	气
系	不	起	再	见

1

 你好

Exercise 4: Create Your Rainbow Character

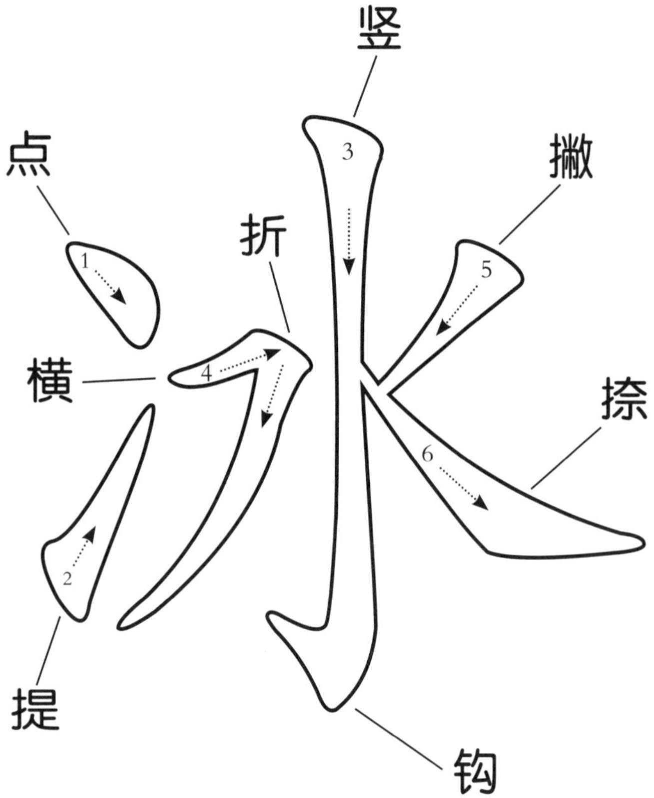

点 diǎn	dot
横 héng	horizontal stroke
竖 shù	vertical stroke
撇 piě	throw stroke
捺 nà	right-falling stroke
提 tí	rising stroke
折 zhé	turning stroke
钩 gōu	hook stroke

The original Chinese characters resembled pictures. They are called pictographs. It took over 3000 years for Chinese characters to evolve into their present-day forms. There are 26 letters in the alphabet of the English language; however, only 8 basic strokes make up all the characters in the Chinese language.

 # 这是什么形状? 2

Exercise 1: Color

Color in the following pictures. Items with the same shape should be colored in the same color.

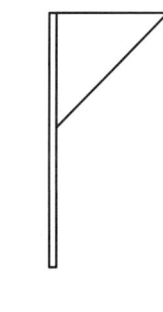

2 这是什么形状？

Exercise 2: Matchmaker
Link the pictures with the correct words.

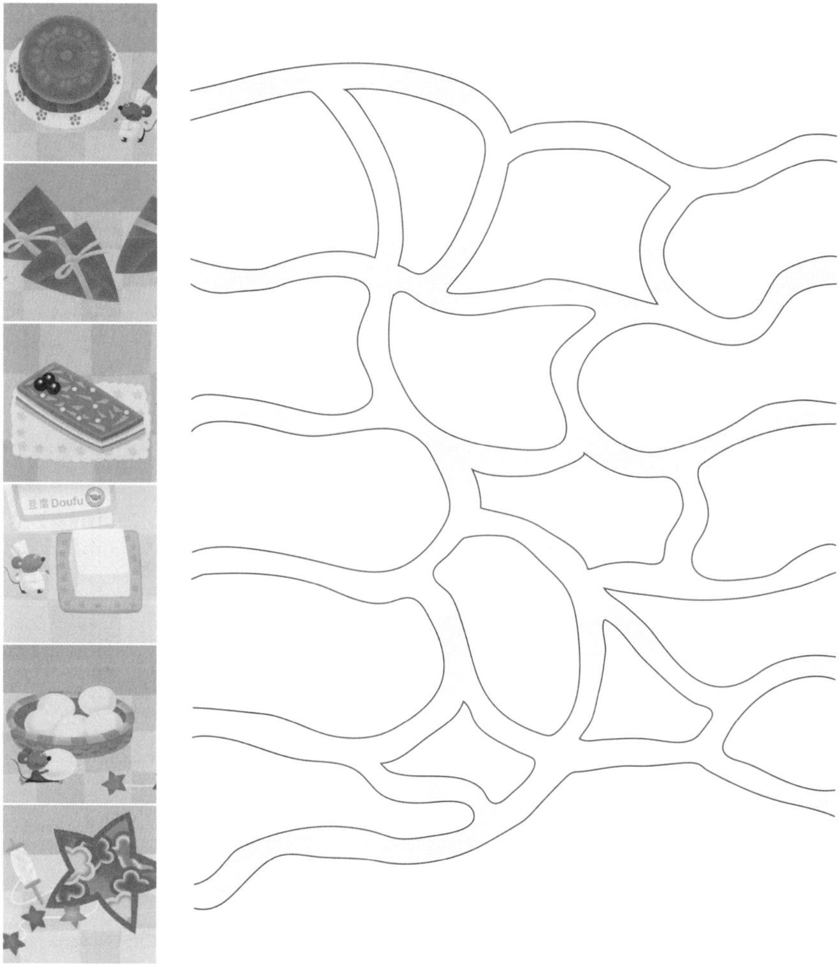

长方形

椭圆形

星形

圆形

正方形

三角形

  # 这是什么形状？ 2

Exercise 3: Happy Face

Draw your happy face with different shapes. Write down your recipe.

Name of Shape	Number Used

Exercise 4: Create Your Rainbow Character

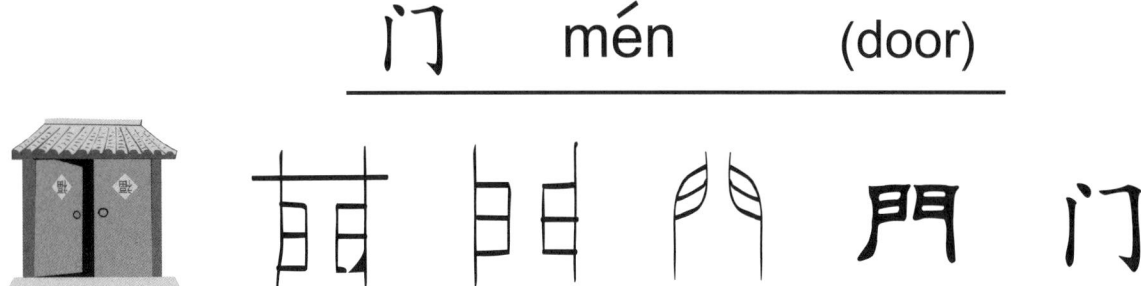

Follow the stroke order and make a rainbow character by using a different color each time.

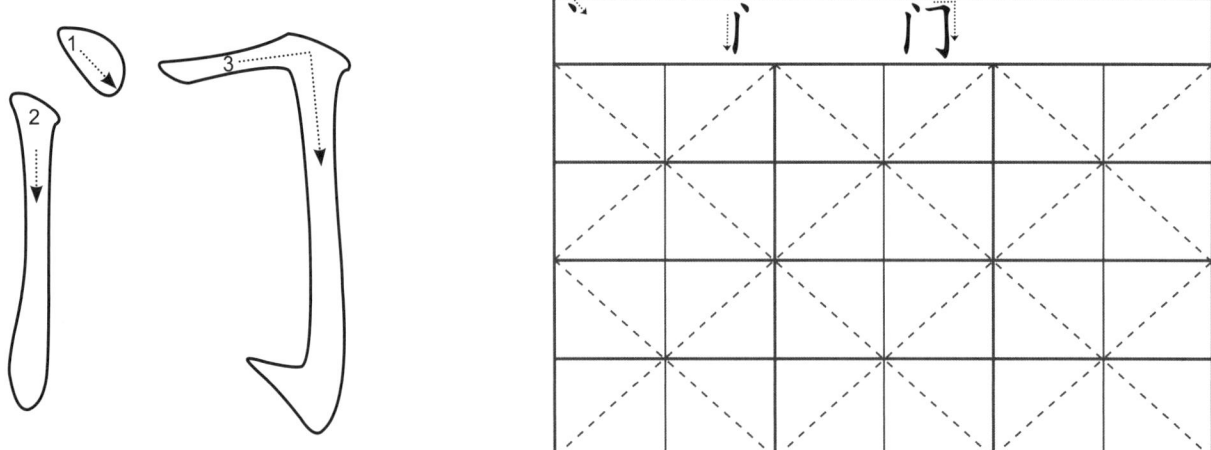

Many of the most frequently used Chinese characters are used to form part of other characters. Such characters are known as "radicals."
Characters with the 门 radical have to do with entrances. Examples: 闭 (to close); 闸 (floodgate); 闯 (to break through a gate).

 你想做什么？

Exercise 1: What Do You Want To Be?

Color in your preference under each picture. Then read your preference and the name of the profession out loud.

   ☺ ☹   

   ☺ ☹

3 你想做什么?

Exercise 2: Matchmaker

Link the pictures with the correct words.

- 医生
- 老师
- 演员
- 厨师
- 警察

 # 你想做什么？

Exercise 3: Drawing

What do you want to be when you grow up? Draw a picture to show us.

Tell your teacher or classmate why you want to do this when you grow up.

Exercise 4: Create Your Rainbow Character

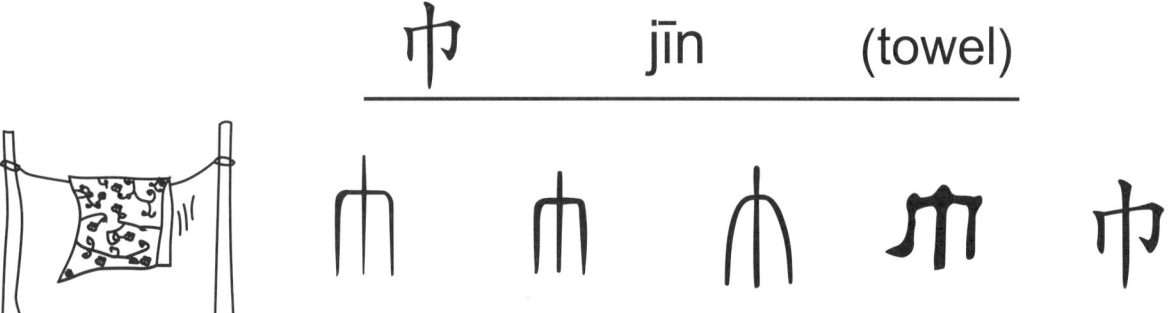

Follow the stroke order and make a rainbow character by using a different color each time.

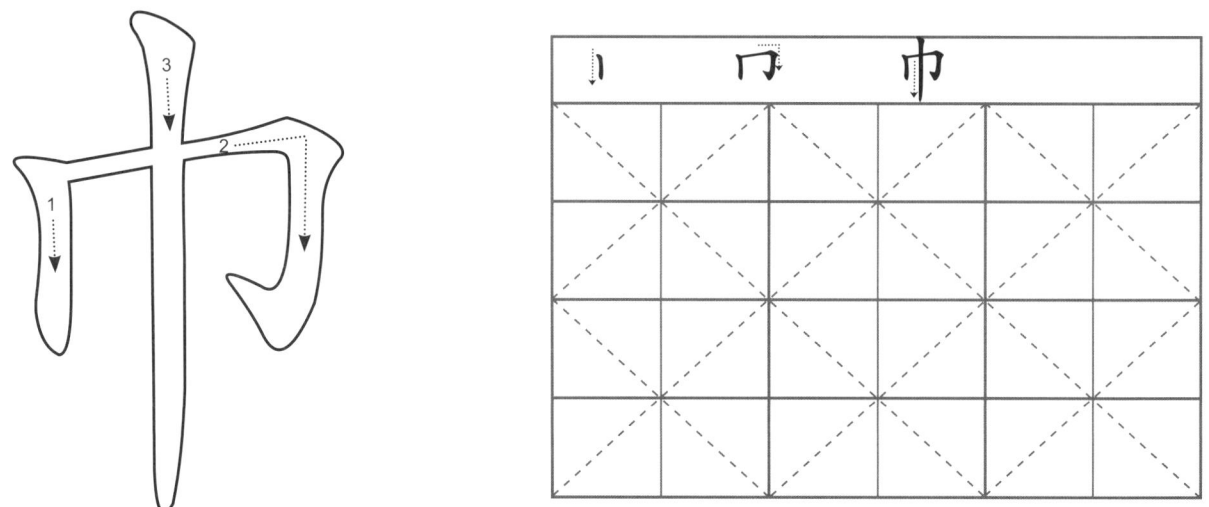

The original pictograph for this character looked like a piece of cloth hung on a line. This character refers primarily to a wash cloth, but it can also be used to refer to a scarf or kerchief. Characters with this radical have to do with cloth. Examples: 布 (cloth); 帘 (curtain); 帽 (hat).

# 你去哪里？

4

Exercise 1: My Way Home
Read the sentences out loud to find your way home.

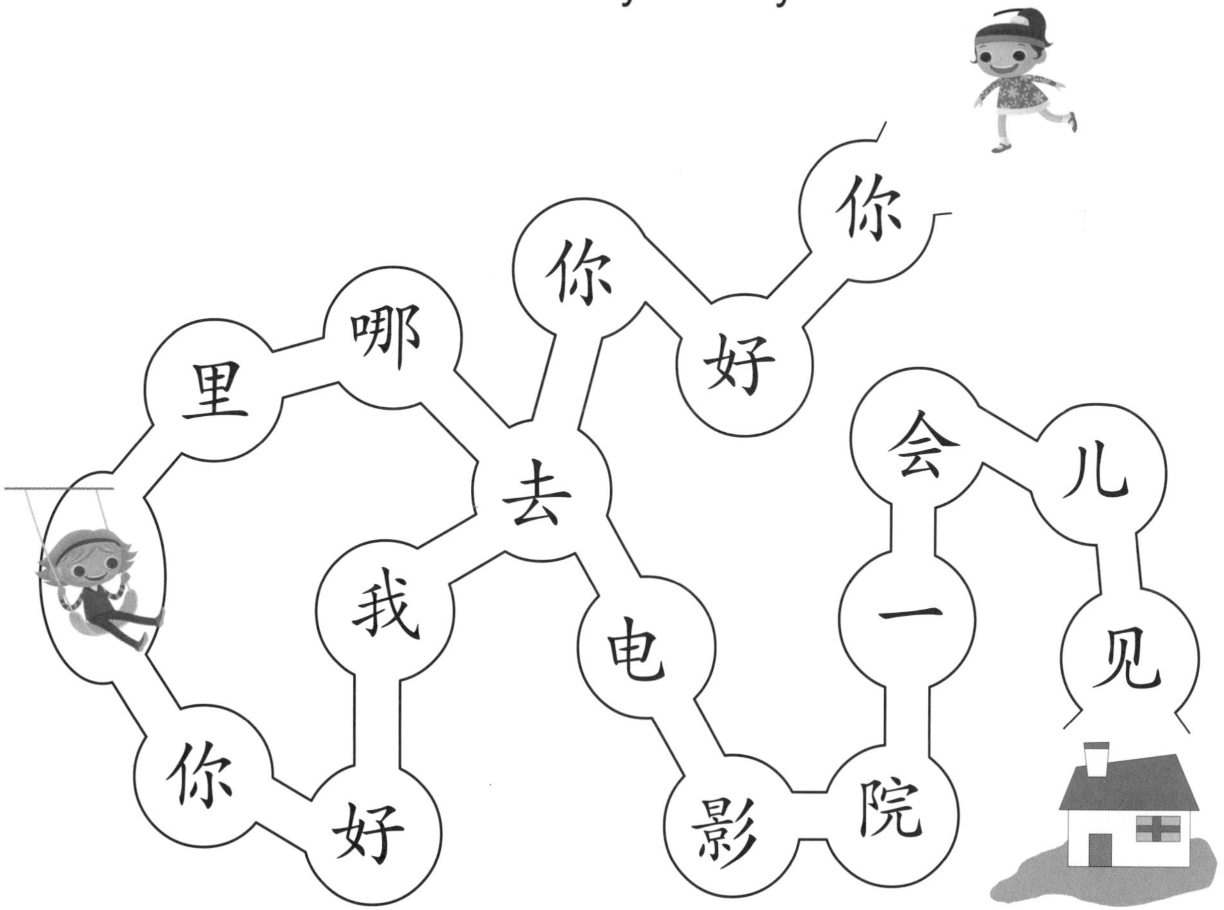

4  你去哪里？

Exercise 2: Where Is It?
Fill in the blanks.

1.电影院　2.餐馆　3.超市　4.游乐场　5.公园　6.学校

你去哪里？

我去_____。　我去_____。　我去_____。

我去_____。　我去_____。　我去_____。

# 你去哪里？

Exercise 3: Mouse's Day
Follow the mouse's thoughts to get through the maze.

我想去：
学校→超市→餐馆→游乐场→电影院

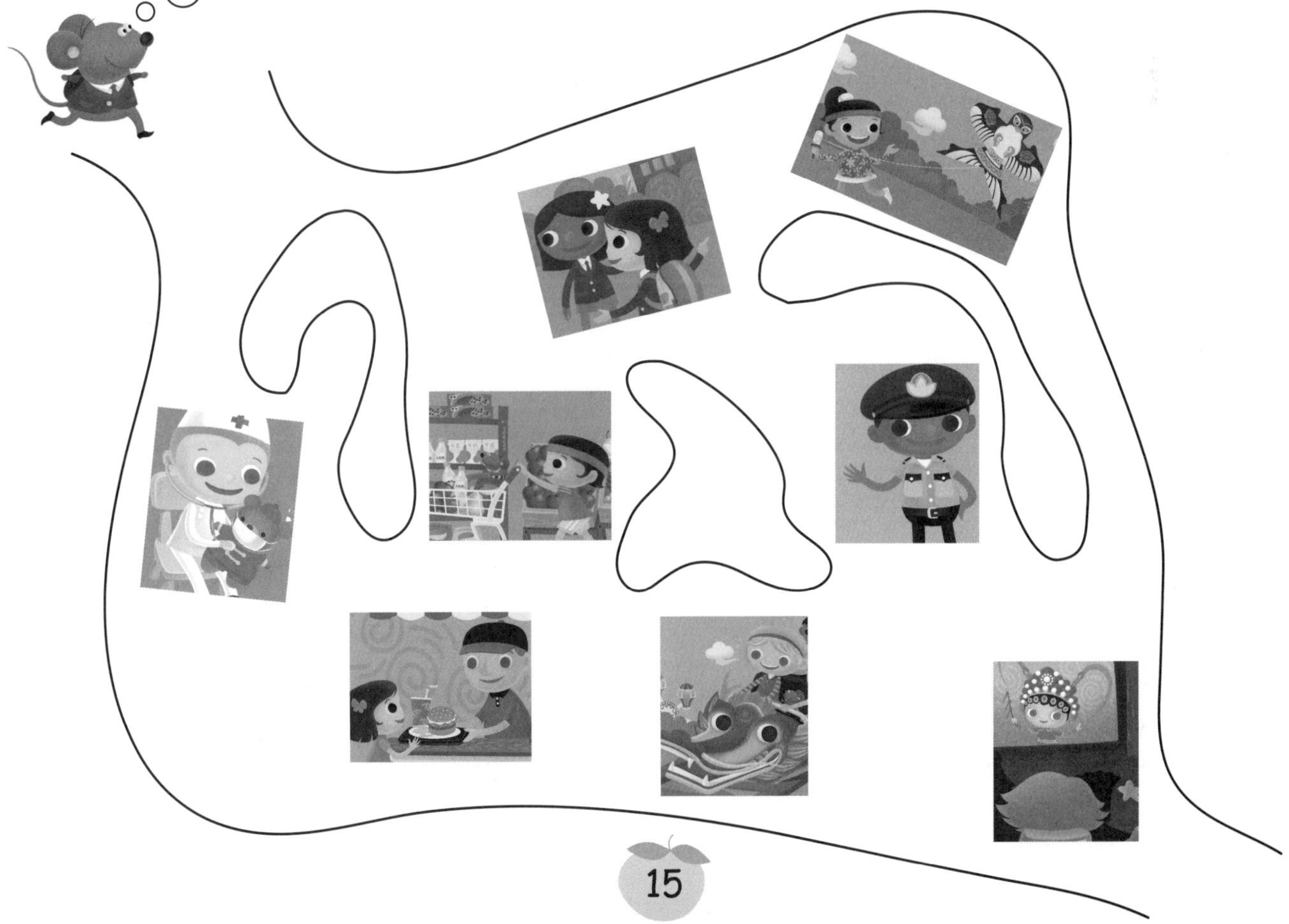

Exercise 4: Create Your Rainbow Character

Follow the stroke order and make a rainbow character by using a different color each time.

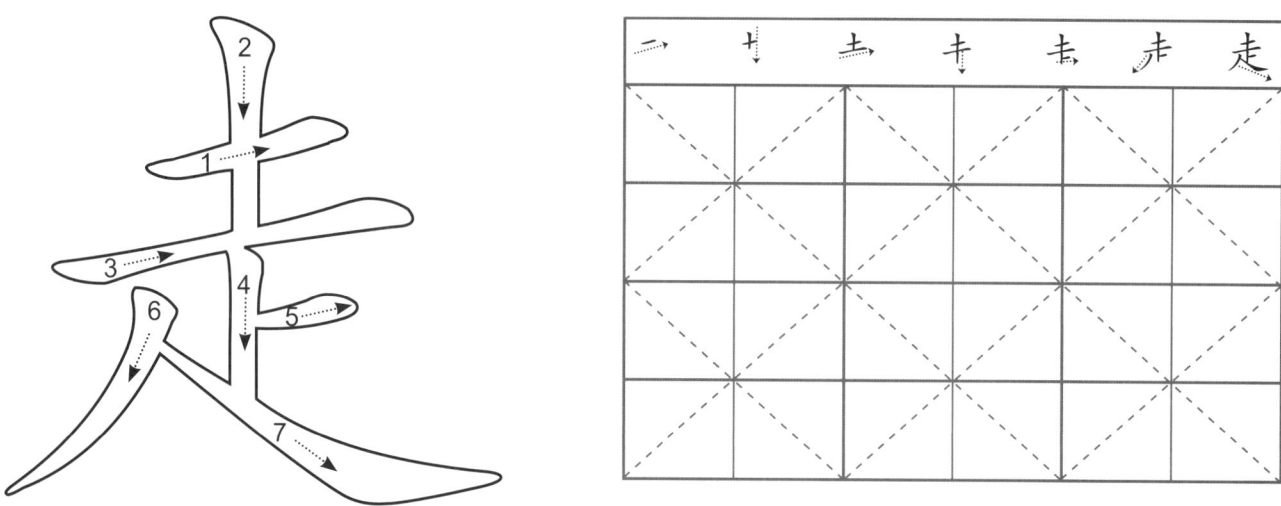

In the ancient Chinese writing system, the top part of this character looks like a man running forward with his arms swinging, while the bottom represents the character for "foot." The original meaning of 走 was "to run," but now this character means "to walk." Characters with this radical usually have to do with running. Examples: 赶 (to rush); 超 (to exceed); 赴 (to go towards).

一年四季

Exercise 1: Categories

Group each item with the corresponding season by writing down its number in the correct space.

⑬ 花谢了　　⑥ (lotus)　　④ (fish)　　⑧ 草绿了　　⑪ (flowers)

② (snowman)　　⑨ 天凉了　　⑩ (bird)

⑫ 虫叫了　　⑤ (lotus pod)

⑭ (snowflake)

⑦ 天热了　　① 下雪了　　③ 天冷了

春天: _____　　夏天: _____

秋天: _____　　冬天: _____

5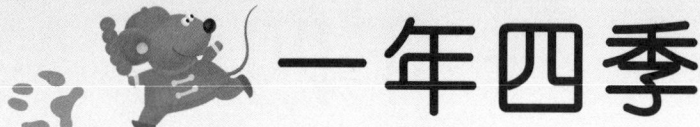

Exercise 2: My Favorite Season

Draw a scene from your favorite season. Then write a short introduction to what you have drawn. You may use Pinyin if necessary.

_____

Read your sentence(s) out loud.

 一年四季

Exercise 3: Nursery Rhyme

Learn the rhyme below.

xiǎo yàn zi chuān huā yī
小燕子穿花衣，

nián nián chūn tiān lái zhè lǐ
年年春天来这里。

wǒ wèn yàn zi nǐ wèi shén me lái
我问燕子你为什么来，

yàn zi shuō　　　zhè lǐ de chūn tiān zuì měi lì
燕子说："这里的春天最美丽！"

Exercise 4: Create Your Rainbow Character

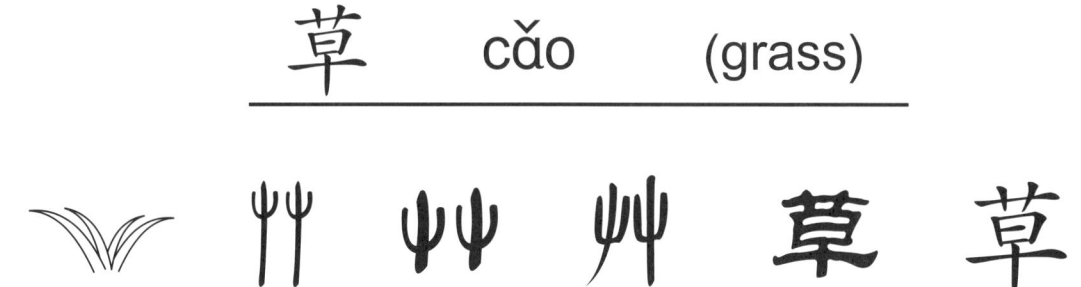

Follow the stroke order and make a rainbow character by using a different color each time.

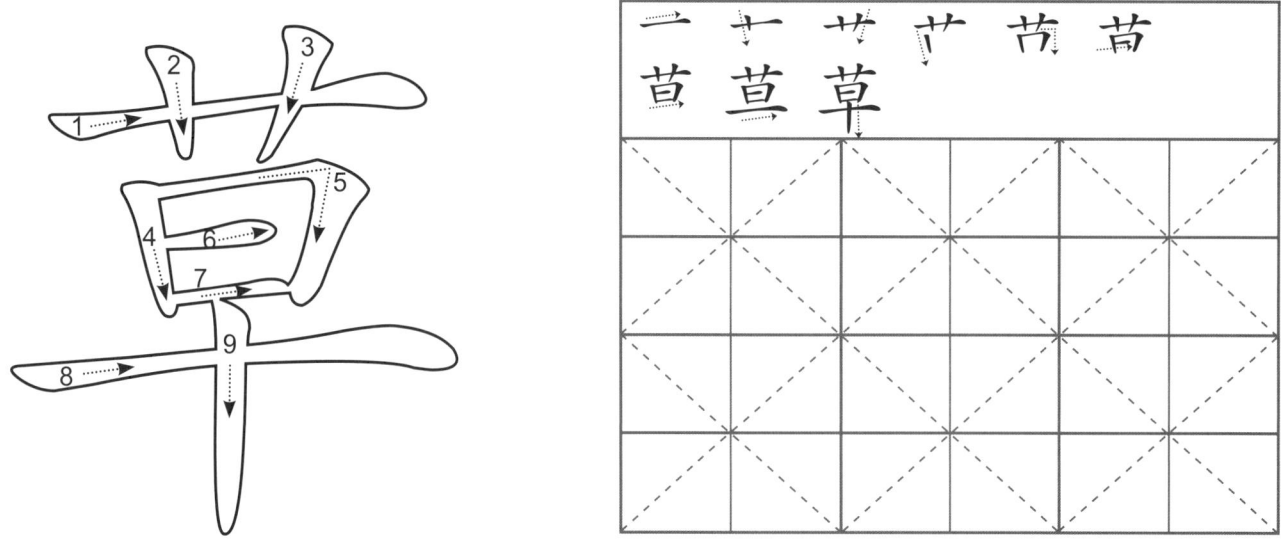

Only the top of the character 草 is used when it is used as a radical. Characters with this radical are usually related to plants. Examples: 苗 (seedling); 花 (flower); 芽 (bud).

真好吃

Exercise 1: Tastes

Circle all the words that describe tastes.

酸 甜 咸 花 香 方 辣 苦 好 绿 热 凉 吃 冷 叫

6 真好吃

Exercise 2: Let's Race!

Use a dice and 4 coins to play this game. Say your number and the action to win the game. Number of players: 1~4

好 甜：move 1 space

真 香：move 2 spaces

真好吃：move 3 spaces

真 咸：skip 1 turn

真 酸：skip 2 turns

好 辣：move back 1 space

真 苦：move back 4 spaces

Start	1	2	3
20	19	18	17
21 真酸			
22	23	24	真好吃 25

 # 真好吃

好甜 **4**	5	6	真咸 **7**	8	9
					10
16	真苦 **15**	14	13	真香 **12**	11
26	27	28	29	好辣 **30**	Win!

6 真好吃

Exercise 3: How Does It Taste?

How do the following foods taste? Cut out the words from page #6.3 in the back of the book and paste them next to foods with that taste.

真酸　好甜　真苦　好辣　真咸　好香

Exercise 4: Create Your Rainbow Character

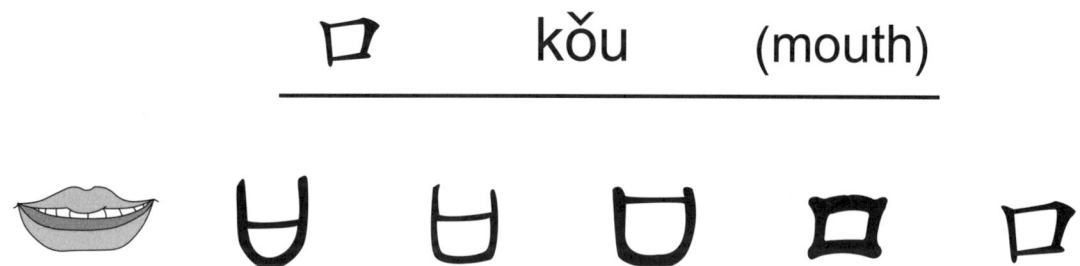

Follow the stroke order and make a rainbow character by using a different color each time.

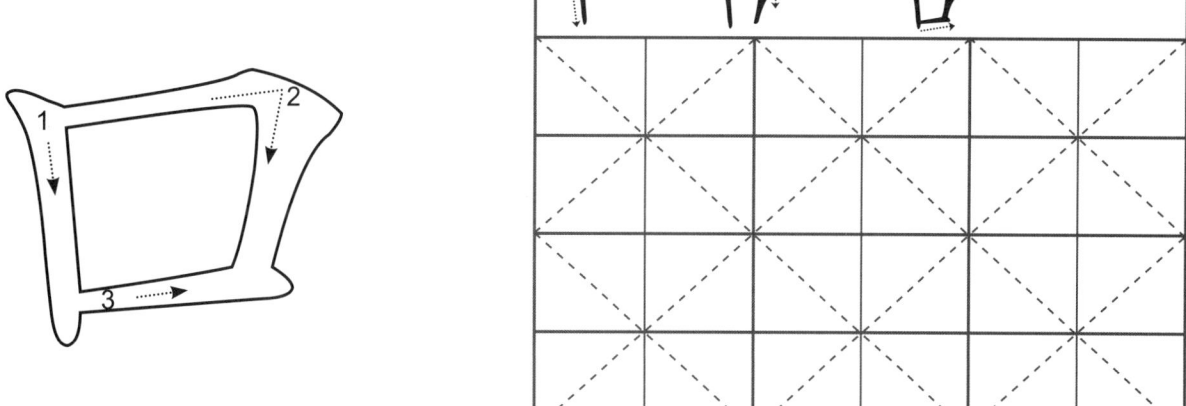

The shape of this character looks like an open mouth of a person or an animal. Characters using the 口 radical usually concern actions that use the mouth. Examples: 吃 (to eat); 叫 (to shout); 吞 (to swallow); 吸 (to suck in).

7   动物

Exercise 1: Animals

Label the animals by matching the numbers with their right names.

长颈鹿 ____

黑熊 ____

狮子 ____

大象 ____

猩猩 ____

大熊猫 ____

  # 动物

Exercise 2: What Did You See？
Answer the question by matching the words with the pictures.

你看到了什么？

1. 电影院

2. 超市

3. 大熊猫

4. 公园

我看到了_____。

我看到了_____。

我看到了_____。

7 动物

Exercise 3: Matchmaker
Color in the animals and link them with their names.

熊猫

狮子   大象

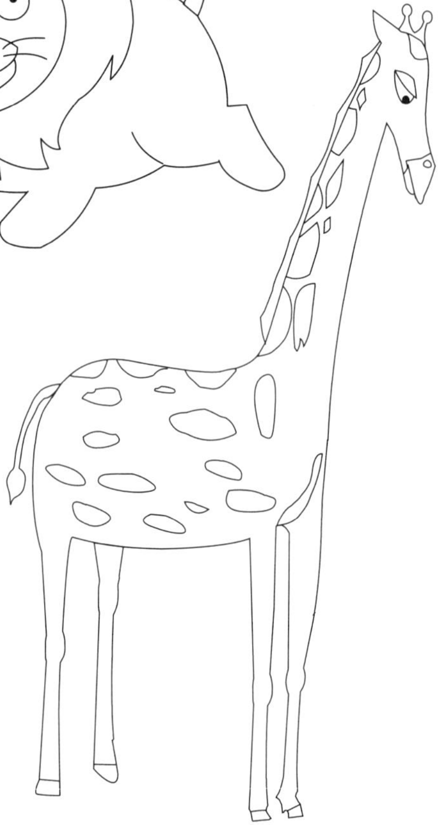

长颈鹿

Exercise 4: Create Your Rainbow Character

犬　　quǎn　　(dog)

Follow the stroke order and make a rainbow character by using a different color each time.

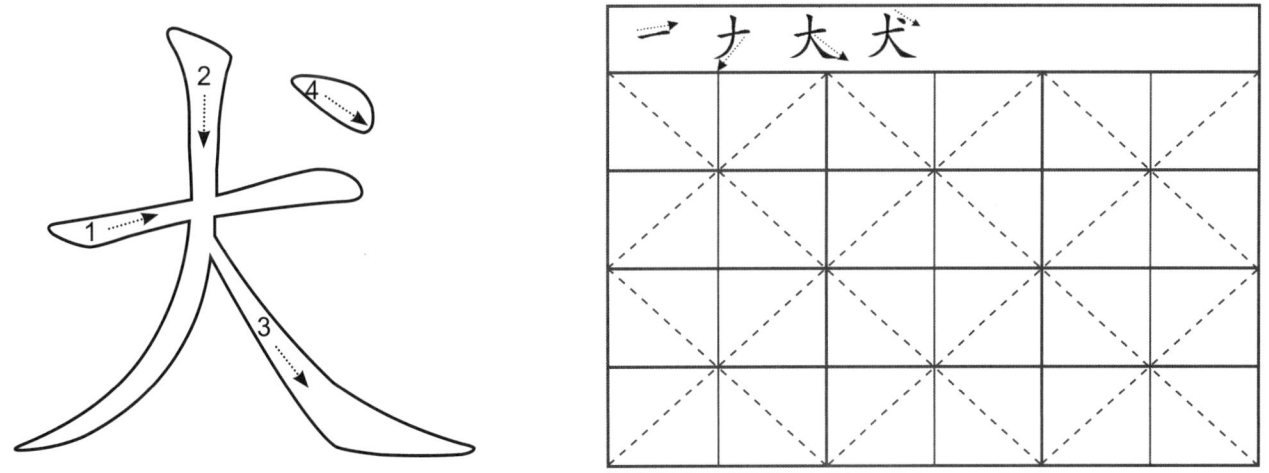

The original character of 犬 was a pictograph of a dog. As a radical it can be written as 犭 or 犭. Most verbs with 犬 have to do with actions related to dogs. Nouns with this radical have to do with animals. Examples: 猎 (to hunt); 狂 ((a dog) going mad); 狐狸 (fox); 猴 (monkey).

8 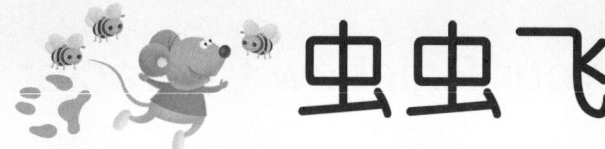 虫虫飞

Exercise 1: Insects, Insects, Insects

Circle the words with radical 虫 on this page. How many can you find?

蚂蚁　　动　　　螳螂

　　虹　　熊　　　　蛇
　　　　　　　　虾
峰
　　椭　　蜻蜓
　　　　　　　　猫　　状
虫　　吃
　　　　　蝴蝶　　　猩猩

_____

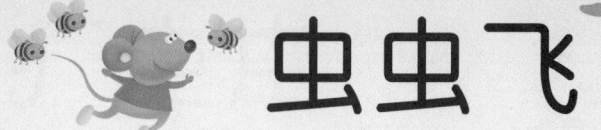 

Exercise 2: Look! What Is It?

Link the two sentences.

看！那是什么？    • 那是蜜蜂。

看！那是什么？    • 那是螳螂。

看！那是什么？    • 那是蚂蚁。

看！那是什么？    • 那是甲虫。

看！那是什么？    • 那是蝴蝶。

8 虫虫飞

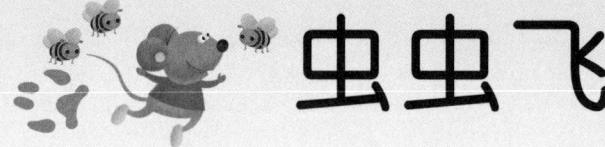

Exercise 3: Puzzle Fun

Circle as many words as you can find.

你	一	年	好	蝴	老	厨
好	吃	起	蜜	超	市	师
蚂	是	季	年	蜂	方	毛
真	蚁	蜻	圆	三	甲	毛
螳	螂	蜓	形	看	吃	虫

6—good! 8—great! 12—wonderful!

Exercise 4: Create Your Rainbow Character

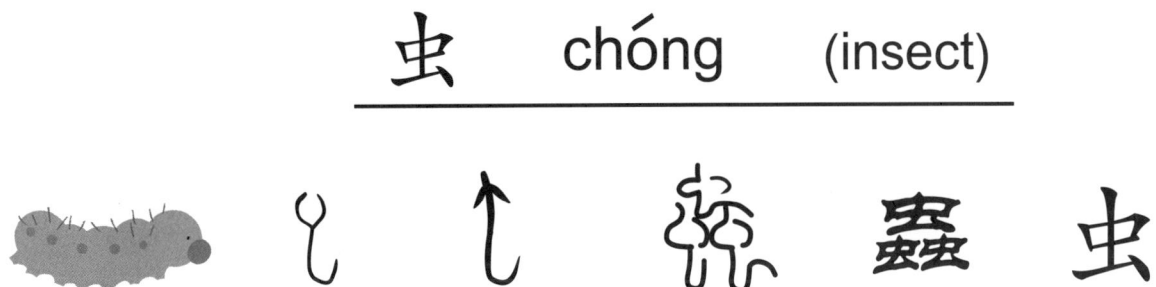

Follow the stroke order and make a rainbow character by using a different color each time.

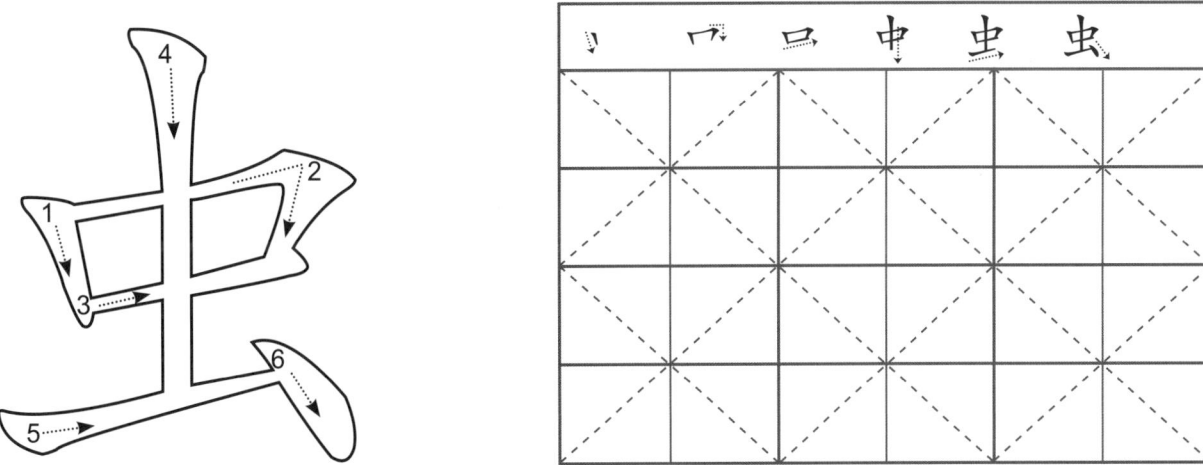

The original pictograph of 虫 resembled the shape of a worm with a pointed head and a curving body. Characters with the radical 虫 have to do with insects, worms and other insects. Examples: 蚊 (mosquito); 蜂 (bee); 蚕 (silkworm).

9 大海里有什么？

Exercise 1: Animals' Homes

Cut out the words from the "cut and paste" page #9.1 at the back of the book. Paste them in the right kind of animal habitat: ocean, grassland or garden.

大象　海豚　鱼　蚂蚁　大熊猫　海龟　黑熊
蜜蜂　狮子　鲸鱼　甲虫　鲨鱼　蜻蜓　长颈鹿
毛毛虫　海狮　蝴蝶　猩猩　海星　螳螂

大海里有什么？

9 大海里有什么？

Exercise 2: Amusing Maze

Follow the directions to lead the animals out of the maze.

Directions:

鱼 → 海星 → 海狮 → 鲨鱼 → 海豚 → 海龟

 # 大海里有什么？

Exercise 3: Fun With Riddles

Write the answer in the box below.

坐(zuò)也是行(xíng)，　　　Sitting is walking.

立(lì)也是行，　　　Standing is walking.

行也是行，　　　Walking is walking.

卧(wò)也是行。　　　Sleeping is walking.

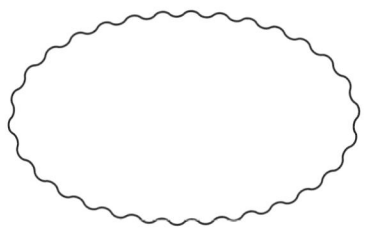

(Guess an animal.)

Exercise 4: Create Your Rainbow Character

鱼   yú   (fish)

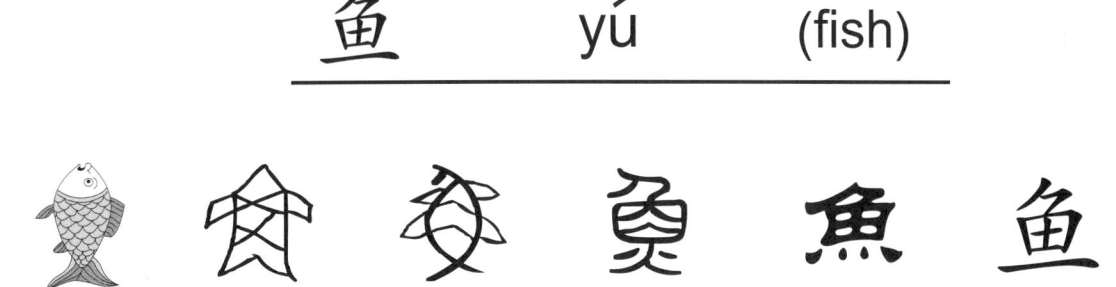

Follow the stroke order and make a rainbow character by using a different color each time.

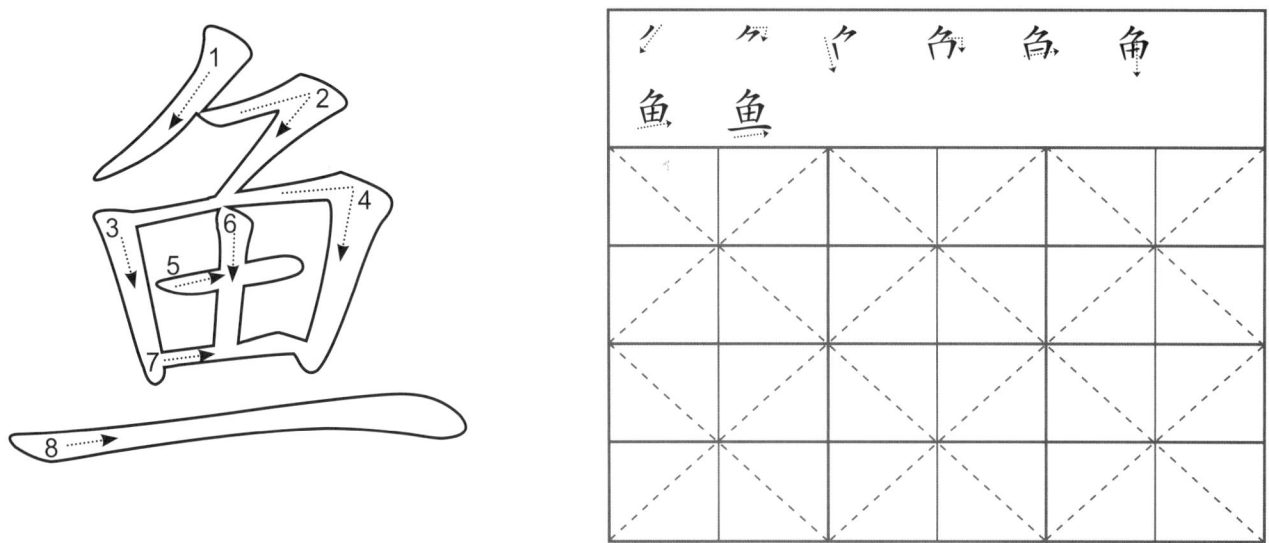

In ancient shell and bone inscriptions, the character 鱼 looks like a fish. Characters with this radical have to do with water animals or their traits. Examples: 鲤 (carp); 鲨 (shark); 鲜 (tasty).

# 我们一起打球

Exercise 1: Invitation

Invite one of your friends to play ball with you.

亲爱的＿＿＿＿：

　　我们下午3点一起去＿＿＿球，好吗？

＿＿＿＿＿
＿＿年＿＿月＿＿日

10 我们一起打球

Exercise 2: Fun With Making Words

Circle all the words that can go with 球. How many can you find?

踢　足　圆　乒乓

　　鱼　春

篮　网

辣　冰　三角

棒

我们一起打球

Exercise 3: Which Is It?

Fill in the appropriate punctuation: ， 。 ！ ？

A: 我们一起打棒球（ ）好吗（ ）

B: 好（ ）

C: 我们一起踢足球（ ）好吗（ ）

D: 对不起（ ）我累了（ ）

Exercise 4: Create Your Rainbow Character

足 zú (foot)

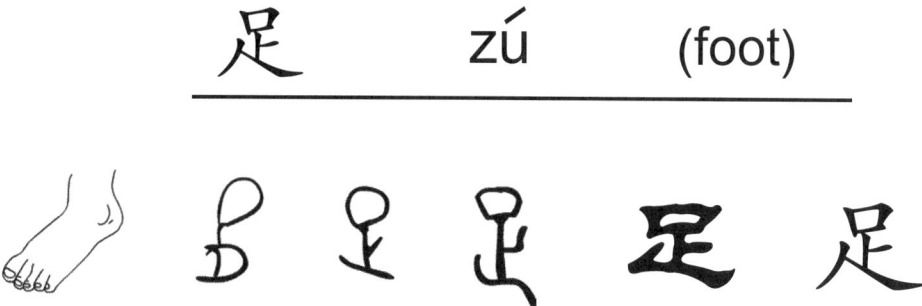

Follow the stroke order and make a rainbow character by using a different color each time.

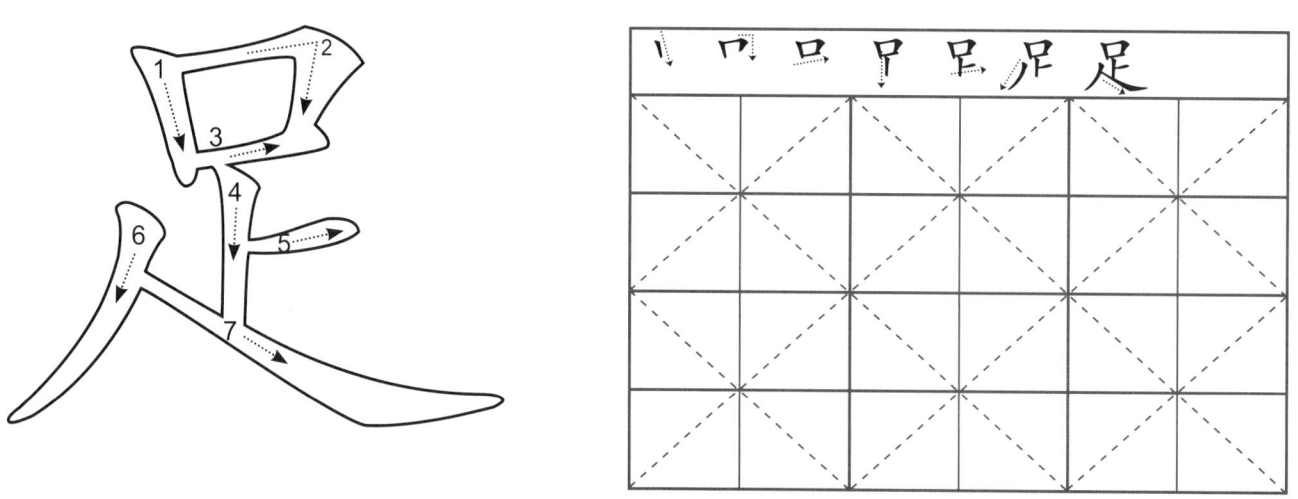

This pictograph resembles a person's foot. The radical can be written as 足 or 足. 足 can be found in characters involving feet and related activities. Examples: 跳 (to jump); 跑 (to run); 跟 (to follow).

我喜欢交朋友

Exercise 1: Likes And Dislikes

Fill in your name, likes and dislikes. Then ask your friends to fill in the additional rows.

Say the sentences "我喜欢____" "我不喜欢____" out loud while you fill in the form.

Name \ Game	捉迷藏	跳房子	滑滑梯	荡秋千	玩跷跷板	交朋友	吵架
Hua hua	☺	☺	☺	☺	☺	☺	☹

11 我喜欢交朋友

Exercise 2: Scrambled Messages
Unscramble the sentences and write out the story.

（1） 1. 跷跷板 2. 喜欢 3. 我 4. 玩

（2） 1. 一起 2. 我们 3. 喜欢 4. 跳房子

（3） 1. 不 2. 喜欢 3. 吵架 4. 我

（1）_____。

（2）_____。

（3）_____。

我喜欢交朋友

Exercise 3: Fun With Tongue Twisters.
Read the sentences below out loud according to the Pinyin.

pèng peng chē　　chē pèng peng
碰　碰　车　，　车　碰　碰　，

zuò zhe péng peng hé píng ping
坐　着　朋　朋　和　平　平　。

píng ping kāi chē pèng péng peng
平　平　开　车　碰　朋　朋　，

péng peng kāi chē pèng píng ping
朋　朋　开　车　碰　平　平　，

bù zhī shì píng ping pèng péng peng
不　知　是　平　平　碰　朋　朋　，

hái shì péng peng pèng píng ping
还　是　朋　朋　碰　平　平　。

Exercise 4: Create Your Rainbow Character

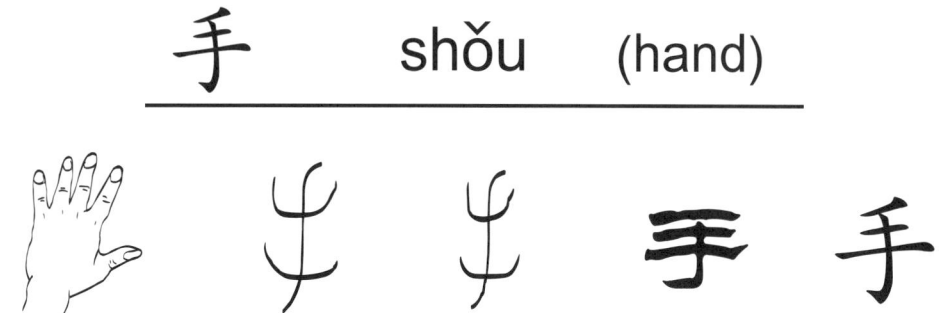

Follow the stroke order and make a rainbow character by using a different color each time.

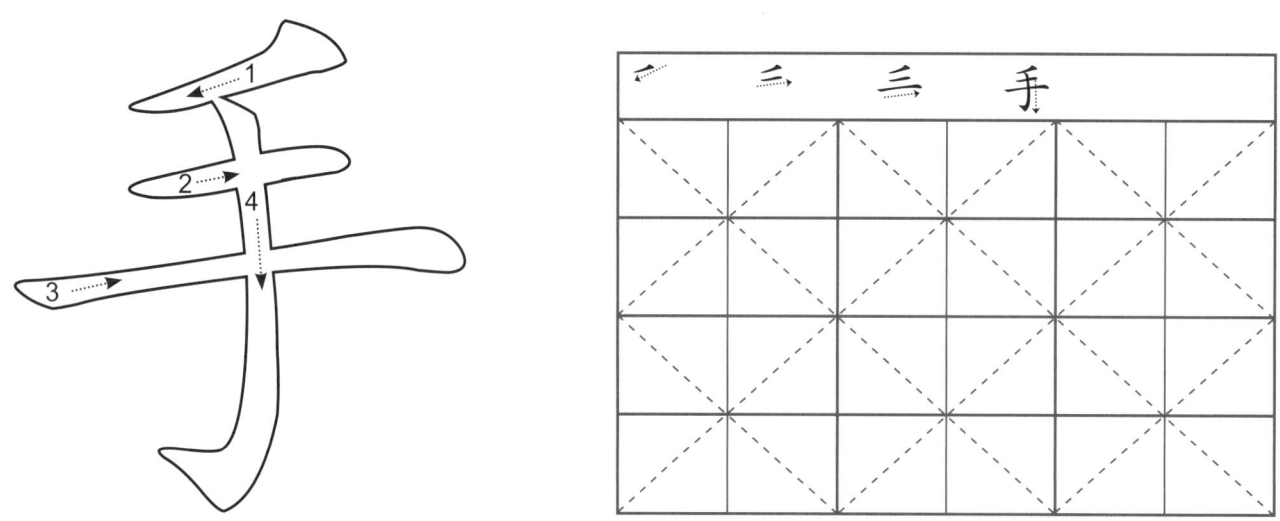

In ancient Chinese writing, 手 resembled a person's hand. The radical is written as 扌. Characters with this radical are related to activities to do with hands. Examples: 拍 (to clap); 打 (to beat); 拉 (to pull).

 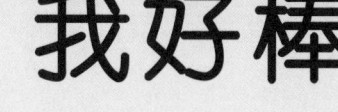

Exercise 1: True Or False

Mark each picture with T or F to show if it is a good habit.

(　　)

(　　)

(　　)

(　　)

(　　)

12 我好棒

Exercise 2: I Am Great!
Write out rules from your school.

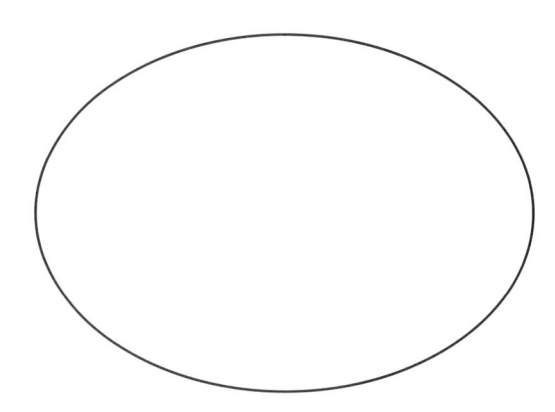

我会先举手，
再说话。

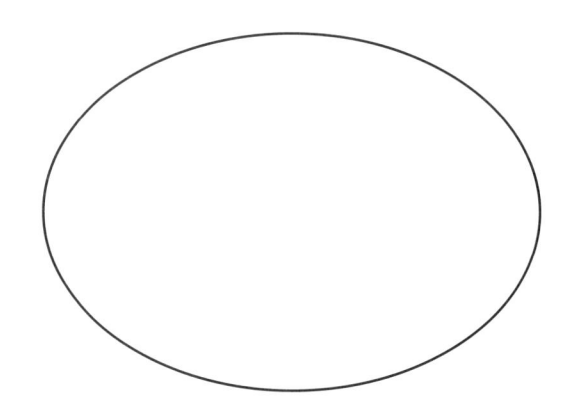

我好棒

Exercise 3: Rhyme

Try to read the rhyme below.

zǎo shang qǐ chuáng shuō shēng zǎo
早上起床说声早，

jiàn dào bié rén wèn shēng hǎo
见到别人问声好；

shàng kè shuō huà xiān jǔ shǒu
上课说话先举手，

lǎo shī diǎn tóu zài zhāng kǒu
老师点头再张口；

dǎ sǎo wèi shēng wǒ lái bāng
打扫卫生我来帮，

wǒ men dōu shì hǎo bāng shǒu
我们都是好帮手！

Exercise 4: Create Your Rainbow Character

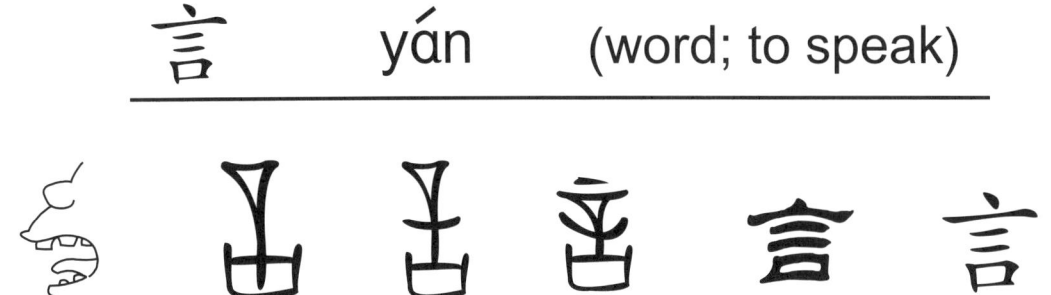

Follow the stroke order and make a rainbow character by using a different color each time.

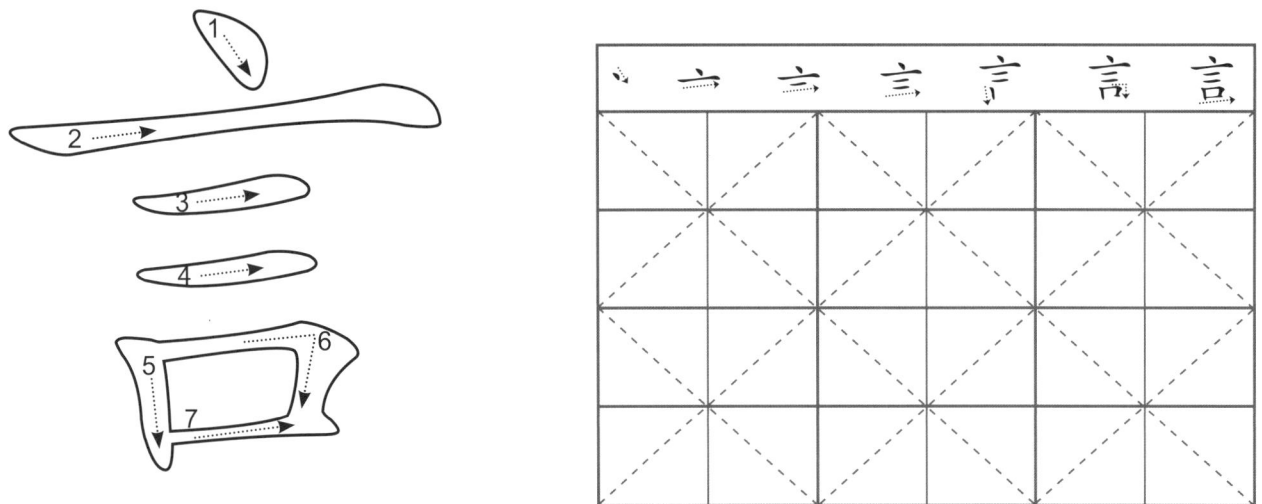

In ancient shell and bone inscriptions, the character 言 resembled a tongue that looked like it was moving. The radical is written as 讠. Characters to do with talking or writing usually have this radical. Examples: 说 (to speak); 读 (to read); 诗 (poem).

Cut and Paste:

#6.3

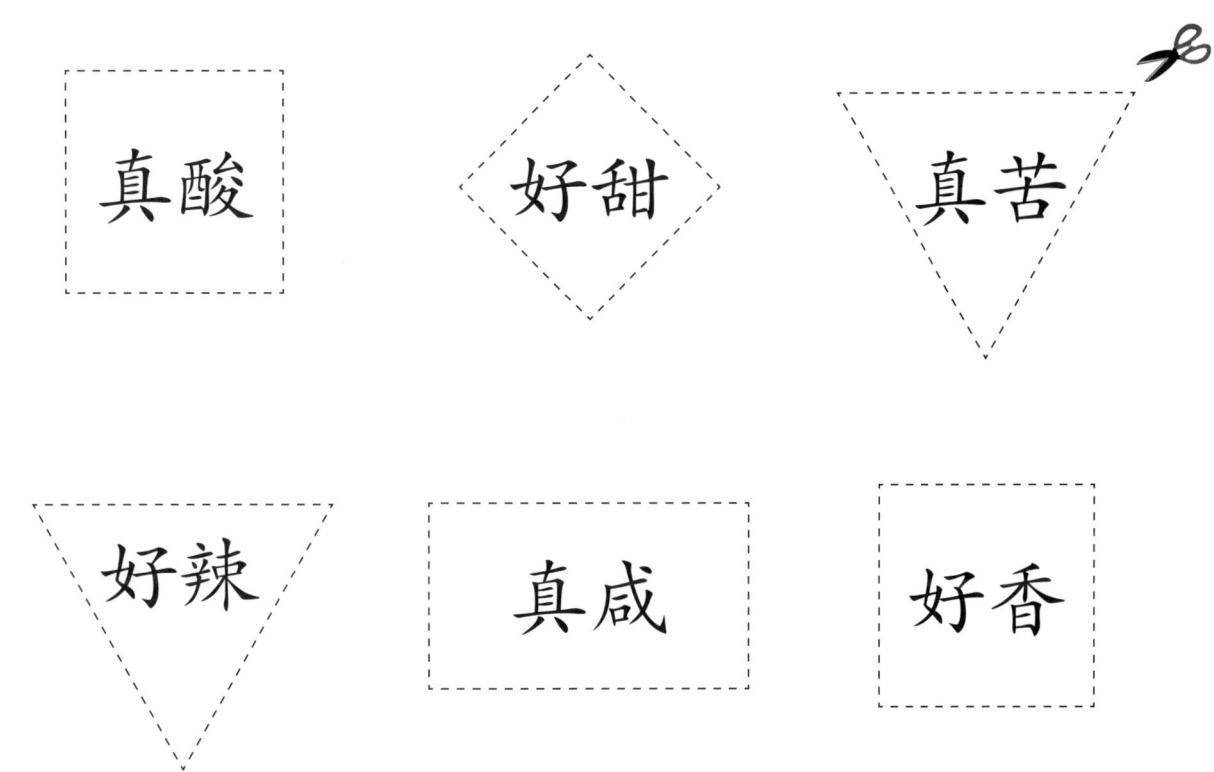

Cut and Paste:

#9.1

大象	海豚	鱼	蚂蚁	大熊猫
海龟	黑熊	螳螂	蜜蜂	狮子
鲸鱼	甲虫	鲨鱼	蜻蜓	长颈鹿
毛毛虫	海狮	蝴蝶	猩猩	海星